MW00442059

# HABITS OF MIND
## Poster Book

**Wonder Media, LLC**

16530 Ventura Boulevard
Suite 600
Encino, CA 91436

1 (800) 8897249

**www.WonderGroveLearn.net**

© 2018 Wonder Media, LLC. All rights reserved.

THE INSTITUTE FOR
## HABITS OF MIND

**Founders and Co-Directors**

Dr. Arthur Costa, Ed. D.
Dr. Bena Kallick, Ph. D.

## wonder media

**Co-Founders**

Terry Thoren
Rudy Verbeeck
Ryan Cannon
Herman Spliethoff
Rita Peeters

# Persisting

I keep trying.

WonderGroveLearn.net

# Managing Impulsivity

I think before I act.

WonderGroveLearn.net

# Listening with Understanding and Empathy

I listen carefully to understand
what someone is saying and feeling.

# Thinking Flexibly

Sometimes I try a different way.

WonderGroveLearn.net

# Thinking About Your Thinking

I'm aware of what I'm thinking.

# Striving for Accuracy

I try many ways to
check my work.

# Questioning and Problem Posing

I ask thoughtful questions.

# Applying Past Knowledge to New Situations

I use what I have learned
in new situations.

WonderGroveLearn.net

# Thinking and Communicating with Clarity & Precision

I choose my words carefully.

# Gathering Data with All Senses

I pay attention to
the world around me.

WonderGroveLearn.net

# Creating, Imagining, & Innovating

I like to use my imagination.

# Responding with Wonderment and Awe

I search for something amazing
in everything I see.

# Taking Responsible Risks

I take safe risks.

C

# Finding Humor

I try to laugh every day.

# Thinking Interdependently

I work well with others.

WonderGroveLearn.net

# Remaining Open to Continuous Learning

I love to learn.

# What is WonderGrove Learn?

The WonderGrove Learn education initiative features engaging animated characters in instructional animations and extension lessons that are aligned to the Common Core State Standards. Lessons are designed for Pre-K, Kindergarten, 1st Grade, and 2nd Grade. Products include WonderGrove and Habits of Mind Animations.

## WonderGrove

WonderGrove covers critical areas of early learning that impact a child's ability to succeed inside and outside of the classroom. These areas of learning include: Social Skills, School Readiness, Life Skills, Health & Science, Safety, Nutrition, Fitness, and Creative Play.

WonderGrove Animations are available in 5 separate formats: **English, Spanish, Arabic, SymbolStix,** assistive captions for students with learning challenges, and **Signing Savvy** for students who are hard of hearing or deaf.

## Habits of Mind Animations

Habits of Mind Animations teach young children critical thinking and problem solving skills using engaging videos and printable extension lessons. Developed with Drs. Art Costa and Bena Kallick of the Institute for Habits of Mind, Habits of Mind Animations includes 16 Instructional Animations on each of the 16 habits, 128 Printable Extension Lessons per grade level, and exclusive resources.

Visit **www.WonderGroveLearn.net** to learn more about about Habits of Mind Animations and WonderGrove products.

For more information about the Institute for Habits of Mind visit: **www.habitsofmindinstitute.org**

**ASCD® PRESENTS**

# HABITS OF MIND
## ANIMATIONS

"Prepare children
for the
tests of life
instead of a life of tests."
- Dr. Bena Kallick

**16** Engaging Animations with **320** Extension Lessons

- Built around the successful Habits of Mind strategies
- Created by Dr. Art Costa and Dr. Bena Kallick
- Models critical thinking and problem-solving
- Designed for students in Pre-K through 2nd grade

Free additional resources available online

DESIGNED
GRAD
PRE K-

To learn more visit us at:
## www.wondergrovelearn.net

**ASCD**
LEARN. TEACH